*GREATER THAN
    ALSO AVAIL.
        AUDIOBOOK FORMAT.

Greater Than a Tourist
Book Series
Reviews from Readers

I think the series is wonderful and beneficial for tourists to get information before visiting the city.

-Seckin Zumbul, Izmir Turkey

I am a world traveler who has read many trip guides but this one really made a difference for me. I would call it a heartfelt creation of a local guide expert instead of just a guide.

-Susy, Isla Holbox, Mexico

New to the area like me, this is a must have!

 -Joe, Bloomington, USA

This is a good series that gets down to it when looking for things to do at your destination without having to read a novel for just a few ideas.

-Rachel, Monterey, USA

Good information to have to plan my trip to this destination.

-Pennie Farrell, Mexico

Great ideas for a port day.

-Mary Martin USA

Aptly titled, you won't just be a tourist after reading this book. You'll be greater than a tourist!

-Alan Warner, Grand Rapids, USA

Even though I only have three days to spend in San Miguel in an upcoming visit, I will use the author's suggestions to guide some of my time there. An easy read - with chapters named to guide me in directions I want to go.

-Robert Catapano, USA

Great insights from a local perspective! Useful information and a very good value!

-Sarah, USA

This series provides an in-depth experience through the eyes of a local. Reading these series will help you to travel the city in with confidence and it'll make your journey a unique one.

-Andrew Teoh, Ipoh, Malaysia

\>TOURIST

GREATER THAN A TOURIST- VIAREGGIO ITALY

50 Travel Tips from a Local

Gabrielle T

Greater Than a Tourist- Viareggio Italy Copyright © 2021 by CZYK Publishing LLC. All Rights Reserved.

All rights reserved. No part of this book may be reproduced in any form or by any electronic or mechanical means including information storage and retrieval systems, without permission in writing from the author. The only exception is by a reviewer, who may quote short excerpts in a review.

The statements in this book are of the authors and may not be the views of CZYK Publishing or Greater Than a Tourist.
First Edition
Cover designed by: Ivana Stamenkovic
Cover Image: https://pixabay.com/photos/viareggio-italy-coast-travel-2425193/

Image 1: By Sailko - Own work, CC BY 3.0,
https://commons.wikimedia.org/w/index.php?curid=85058106
Image 2: By Sailko - Own work, CC BY 2.5,
https://commons.wikimedia.org/w/index.php?curid=1329904
Image 3: By Sailko - Own work, CC BY 2.5,
https://commons.wikimedia.org/w/index.php?curid=1329935
Image 4: By Sailko - Own work, CC BY 2.5,
https://commons.wikimedia.org/w/index.php?curid=1329939

CZYK
PUBLISHING

CZYK Publishing Since 2011.
CZYKPublishing.com
Greater Than a Tourist

Lock Haven, PA
All rights reserved.
ISBN: 9798413966549

>TOURIST
50 TRAVEL TIPS FROM A LOCAL

BOOK DESCRIPTION

With travel tips and culture in our guidebooks written by a local, it is never too late to visit Viareggio. Greater Than a Tourist-Viareggio by Gabrielle T. offers the inside scoop on the Pearl of the Versilia Mediterranean. Most travel books tell you how to travel like a tourist. Although there is nothing wrong with that, as part of the 'Greater Than a Tourist' series, this book will give you candid travel tips from someone who has lived at your next travel destination. This guide book will not tell you exact addresses or store hours but instead gives you knowledge that you may not find in other smaller print travel books. Experience cultural, culinary delights, and attractions with the guidance of a Local. Slow down and get to know the people with this invaluable guide. By the time you finish this book, you will be eager and prepared to discover new activities at your next travel destination.

Inside this travel guide book you will find:

Visitor information from a Local
Tour ideas and inspiration
Valuable guidebook information

Greater Than a Tourist- A Travel Guidebook with 50 Travel Tips from a Local. Slow down, stay in one place, and get to know the people and culture. By the time you finish this book, you will be eager and prepared to travel to your next destination.

\>TOURIST

OUR STORY

Traveling is a passion of the Greater than a Tourist book series creator. Lisa studied abroad in college, and for their honeymoon Lisa and her husband toured Europe. During her travels to Malta, an older man tried to give her some advice based on his own experience living on the island since he was a young boy. She was not sure if she should talk to the stranger but was interested in his advice. When traveling to some places she was wary to talk to locals because she was afraid that they weren't being genuine. Through her travels, Lisa learned how much locals had to share with tourists. Lisa created the Greater Than a Tourist book series to help connect people with locals. A topic that locals are very passionate about sharing.

>TOURIST

TABLE OF CONTENTS

Book Description

Our Story

Table of Contents

Dedication

About the Author

How to Use This Book

From the Publisher

WELCOME TO > TOURIST

1. Visit During Carnevale
2. Tour The Liberty Buildings
3. Get Your Summer Glow On
4. Be Ready For Crowds
5. Make It Homebase
6. Enjoy The Neighborhood Markets (145)
7. Explore Its Opera History
8. If You're Renting A Car, Be Ready To Pay For Parking
9. Have Cash On Hand
10. Stay Near The Beach To Be Close To The Nightlife
11. Consider Renting An Apartment
12. If You're Taking The Bus, Don't Be A Stickler For Time
13. Learn About The Fishing History

14. Be Ready For The Heat
15. You Can Definitely Hoof It
16. Don't Expect Much English
17. Dress Up A Little
18. But You Don't Have To Exaggerate
19. Visit The Lake
20. Don't Miss The Cittadella
21. I Hope You Like Fish
22. Go For A Long Walk On The Beach
23. Careful Of The Jellyfish
24. ...And The Weever Fish
25. Go On A Gelato Crawl
26. Don't Expect Snow
27. Get Used To The Business Hours
28. Don't Skip Merenda
29. Be Prepared To Eat...A Lot
30. Be Ready For Some Old School Ways Of Life
31. Don't Rely On The Wi-Fi
32. Take In A Show
33. Decide Your Budget Based On Location
34. Head To Camaiore For A Mountain Escape
35. Support A Local Artist
36. Pick Your Favorite Cafe
37. Head To The Arcade For Some Nostalgia
38. Have An Aperitivo
39. Don't Forget The Pizza

40. Bring The Whole Family
41. Watch Out For Wild Boar
42. Get Ready To Take It Easy
43. Have Some Seasonal Treats
44. You Might Find Confetti Everywhere
45. Don't Expect Many Non-Italian Options
46. Get Out On The Water
47. See The Lotus Marshes
48. Go Bird Watching
49. Become A Soccer Fan
50. Don't Be Afraid To Chat With The Locals

TOP REASONS TO BOOK THIS TRIP

Other Resources:

Packing and Planning Tips

Travel Questions

Travel Bucket List

NOTES

>TOURIST

DEDICATION

This book is dedicated to my family who always made sure I knew the beauty of home.

ABOUT THE AUTHOR

Gabrielle T. is a writer, translator, and a bona-fide Italian through and through. Born in the Midwest, she moved to Italy as a child and has lived in the Viareggio area for her entire adult life. Gabrielle lives with her two cats while she pursues her careers in writing and translating, with a little teaching thrown in for good measure. She has a degree in psychology from the British OU. She loves to travel and explore everywhere the world has to offer, but it's always nice to come back home.

>TOURIST

HOW TO USE THIS BOOK

The *Greater Than a Tourist* book series was written by someone who has lived in an area for over three months. The goal of this book is to help travelers either dream or experience different locations by providing opinions from a local. The author has made suggestions based on their own experiences. Please check before traveling to the area in case the suggested places are unavailable.

Travel Advisories: As a first step in planning any trip abroad, check the Travel Advisories for your intended destination.
https://travel.state.gov/content/travel/en/traveladvisories/traveladvisories.html

\>TOURIST

FROM THE PUBLISHER

Traveling can be one of the most important parts of a person's life. The anticipation and memories that you have are some of the best. As a publisher of the Greater Than a Tourist, as well as the popular *50 Things to Know* book series, we strive to help you learn about new places, spark your imagination, and inspire you. Wherever you are and whatever you do I wish you safe, fun, and inspiring travel.

Lisa Rusczyk Ed. D.
CZYK Publishing

>TOURIST

WELCOME TO
> TOURIST

>TOURIST

A view of one of Viareggio's Hotel Royal along the passeggiata ("promenade"), with the "Fountain of the Four Seasons" by Beppe Domenici in front.

The Burlamacca canal and the old lighthouse.

Torre Matilde and the Marina of Lucca.

*Villa Borbone, between Viareggio and
Torre del Lago Puccini.*

> TOURIST

"To travel is to live."

-Hans Christian Anderson

Viareggio is one of those cities that most people don't know about, but once you've been there, you can't imagine a time when you weren't aware of its existence. It's a hit vacation spot among tourists from parts of Europe, but much of the world is still unaware of this pearl of a city on the Tuscan coast. As someone who has called Viareggio home for a decade, I can tell you that it deserves to be on more people's radar. Viareggio is a city that's full of art, culture, beauty, and so much more.

If you're looking to take a vacation in the Summer, you can be sure to enjoy the miles of soft, sandy beaches that Viareggio has to offer by day and the multitude of shows, concerts, and events on the seafront by night. If a winter trip is more your speed, then Viareggio still has plenty for you. Come during Carnevale and see the giant paper mache floats, hop on over to the Torre del Lago neighborhood to get in some opera history.

When you're in Viareggio, you're just a hop, skip, and a jump from anywhere in Tuscany you could ever want to visit, but Viareggio has got more than enough to keep you busy. All the more reason it should be at the top of your travel bucket list.

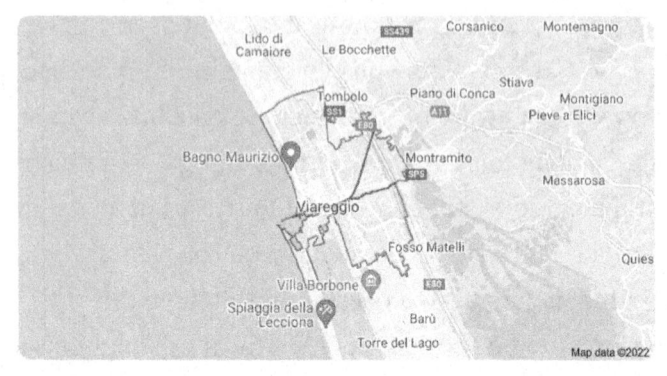

Viareggio
55049 Province of Lucca, Italy

Viareggio Italy Climate

	High	Low
January	55	36
February	55	36
March	60	40
April	65	45
May	72	52
June	80	58
July	85	63
August	85	64
September	79	58
October	70	52
November	60	44
December	53	37

GreaterThanaTourist.com

Temperatures are in Fahrenheit degrees.
Source: NOAA

>TOURIST
1. VISIT DURING CARNEVALE

You might be familiar with the Carnevale in Venice, but Viareggio's Carnevale is a whole different story. While you'll still catch locals dressing up in costume for the occasion, there's a more whimsical vibe to the event. Most people dress in animal costumes to fight against the late winter chill since the main events of Carnevale are the parades. Giant paper-mache floats roll down the seafront promenade blaring music that just makes the whole thing one giant party. The floats are works of art in and of themselves, but they go one step further, what makes them really memorable is their message. The Viareggio Carnevale is a way for artists to use satire to portray public opinion on political topics of all sorts. From pollution to remembering historical figures to current events. You'll see it all at Carnevale!

Carnevale is at the heart of Viareggio's culture and it's the city's biggest annual event. It happens every year in the weeks before lent, so, unfortunately, you can't go the same days every year and know for sure you'll be able to catch it. Don't worry, the dates are decided well in advance, so you're just a quick search away.

2. TOUR THE LIBERTY BUILDINGS

Viareggio's seafront promenade is the best spot to go for a stroll in the whole city. Not only will you be among the locals and really blend in, but it's also gorgeous. Most of the buildings that line the promenade are built in the "liberty" architecture style which is characterized by a lot of intricate external details. Each building is like a work of art and it gives the sea an interesting vibe that you won't see anywhere else. You'll honestly feel like you have one foot in the present and one in the past, but I mean that in the best possible way! There are other liberty style buildings scattered throughout Viareggio, too, so you can take a whole day just meandering through town to find them all. Want a recommendation? The Margherita, which is now a restaurant and bookstore, is one of the biggest and most ornate, definitely worth a few picture perfect moments!

>TOURIST

3. GET YOUR SUMMER GLOW ON

If you don't go to Viareggio for Carnevale, then you have to go during the summer. As a coastal city, the locals take the beach very seriously. I mean incredibly seriously. You'll be hard-pressed to find a local "viareggino" who doesn't find time to lounge on the beach. If you're on the paler side, like me, you'll definitely want to make sure you pack sunscreen, because you'll end up on the beach. It's sort of like a Twilight Zone effect, whether intentionally or not, you'll end up by the water. It's the perfect place to come if you're looking to work on your tan, between the marble seafront paving that reflects the sun's rays and just laying out on the beach, you'll develop a nice, healthy glow, even if you make sure to have plenty of SPF 50 slathered on.

4. BE READY FOR CROWDS

So, you've decided to head to Viareggio, great! If you travel at any point during Carnevale or the summer, however, you're going to have to brace yourself for some crowds. Viareggio has been a popular tourist spot among Italians from all over the country and Europeans in general, and the beach is a huge draw. You don't have to worry about Time Square types of crowds, but you'll definitely notice more people than you might in other small hamlets.

You'll have to look out in particular if you come during August. That's the biggest vacation month for Italians, not only will you have to contend with out of towners, but you'll also be dealing with more locals than at other times of the year. I recommend leaving behind any notions about getting things done quickly, you'll have to wait in longer lines and for longer amounts of time. Another big tip? Make reservations any time you can, you'll thank me for that.

5. MAKE IT HOMEBASE

You know what a great part about Viareggio is? Its location. Not just because of the beach, though that's a big check in the pro column of Viareggio's pro/con list. It's centrally located to offer you the perfect homebase if you want to venture into other parts of Tuscany. The Viareggio train station is considered a bit of a hub and you can easily catch a direct train to Florence, Pisa, Lucca, and more. What's more, if the train isn't exactly your thing, you can catch a bus to most places as well, all that leave from Viareggio's main bus port in Piazza D'Azeglio, right off the promenade. Even branching out of Tuscany isn't the headache you think it might be if you stay in Viareggio.

If you're looking to check off a few places on your Italy must-visit list, you likely won't find a better place to find a homebase than Viareggio. The city is even safe after dark, so you don't have to worry about cutting your day trips off early to head back to your home away from home.

6. ENJOY THE NEIGHBORHOOD MARKETS (145)

No matter what time of year you visit, Viareggio will have neighborhood markets, or "mercati rionali", for you to browse. These markets are a staple in every Italian city and date back to when they were the only way for people to get what they needed from vendors and merchants.

Now, with cars, big box stores, and supermarkets, people have options of where to shop, but the markets are still a huge part of Italian culture. You can find produce, clothes, and much more at the weekly markets. The most popular of the weekly Viareggio markets is right along the promenade where you'll find dozens of booths for you to peruse.

If you come during some special times of year, around Christmas or during certain periods in the summer, you'll also be able to find, in addition to the weekly markets, special pop-up markets full of vintage and antique or artisanal goods. The Viareggio markets truly are the best place for you to pick up a few souvenirs so you can remember your trip.

>TOURIST

7. EXPLORE ITS OPERA HISTORY

Whether or not you're an opera buff yourself, there's no way you can come to Viareggio without getting a little crash course in how deeply opera is woven into Viareggio's culture. Why, you may ask? Well, take a little ride over to Torre Del Lago, a "frazione" or neighborhood in Viareggio and you'll find out!

Torre Del Lage was home to the famous Puccini for years. In fact, you can even take a guided tour of the house he resided in right on the lake. If you come during the summer, you'll likely be able to catch some of the Festival Puccini. During that time you'll find programs for some of his most famous operas you can get tickets for and enjoy. That's not all, though! There are themed 5k runs, concerts, and a spattering of other events that really show how important Puccini and opera are to Viareggio.

8. IF YOU'RE RENTING A CAR, BE READY TO PAY FOR PARKING

So, you've decided renting a car is the way you want to get around while you're staying in Viareggio. It's a good choice. You can easily zip on over to Lido di Camaiore, Forte dei Marmi, Pietrasanta, just to name a few of the neighboring towns, not to mention the convenience of taking your time going to cities further. Even just getting around Viareggio can be more convenient with a car.

However, be warned, depending on your loghings, you may not have parking included in your stay. Not all the hotels have their own parking areas and the same goes for apartments. That means you'll have to street park. Which, unfortunately, means you'll likely have to pay for parking if you stay in some of the most popular areas that are closer to the sites.

An all-day pass will run you around €10 if you plan on being parked in the same spot all day. It's also worth noting that Viareggio is divided into "zones" for parking, so you can't use the parking pass from one zone in another. On the bright side, once you get

>TOURIST

the hang of the ticket dispensers and how to key in the amount of time you want, it's like second nature!

9. HAVE CASH ON HAND

You might be used to not having to carry much cast around with you in your day-to-day life, and that sort of mentality can get you by pretty well in some larger Italian cities, unfortunately, Viareggio isn't one of them just yet. If you're shopping at one of the boutiques or eating at a restaurant, relying on your debit or credit card won't be an issue, just make sure your card provider is on the list of accepted cards, just like anywhere else.

However, if you're looking to buy something from one of the market booths or you want to grab a quick breakfast at a cafe like a local, or a bite to eat at a sandwich truck you might see parked around, cash is going to be your best friend. You shouldn't need much, around €50 should be fine as a baseline amount to have with you in actual, physical, money.

10. STAY NEAR THE BEACH TO BE CLOSE TO THE NIGHTLIFE

If you want to be up close and personal with the nightlife in Viareggio without having to depend on one of the dance clubs, staying near the beach is your best option. During the summer the shops and restaurants are open until midnight at the earliest and you'll definitely hear and see people walking around well into the night. Most of the city's summer shows and events, especially those that don't require tickets, will happen on the promenade as well.

During the winter businesses all over the city close a bit earlier, but those on the promenade stay open a little longer, so on the weekend you'll still see plenty of people walking around. If you're looking for a little nighttime excitement that's fit for people of all ages, then pick a hotel or vacation rental near the beach.

11. CONSIDER RENTING AN APARTMENT

If you're intending to stay in Viareggio, instinct might tell you to check out hotels first. That's definitely a solid option, there are plenty to choose from. However, Viareggio has had vacation apartment rentals available since long before Airbnb existed. You'll find the most options during the summer, but all year round there are apartments just waiting to be a vacationing party's home away from home.

True, it may cost more than a hotel, but think about the trade off. You get your own kitchen, more space, sometimes your own garden. You also have more options as far as where you can stay. Most of the hotels are centered on the promenade, if you decide to go for an apartment rental, you'll find options in all the quaint and characteristic areas of Viareggio. If you don't mind not having turn-down service and you want a little more privacy on your trip, especially if you're traveling as a family or group, a vacation apartment might be the best route for your Viareggio stay.

12. IF YOU'RE TAKING THE BUS, DON'T BE A STICKLER FOR TIME

Maybe you decided that you'd rather take the bus around Viareggio. It's a small city, you're never too far away from anything, so the bus is definitely a good option. However, if you're rushing to a reservation, you may want to build in some extra time to get to where you need to go.

The Viareggio buses are pretty reliable, you likely won't have any huge waits, especially if you hop on a bus at the main depot near the promenade, but delays are definitely possible, if not likely. Taking the bus in Viareggio is a great way to learn to let go if you're usually a stickler about time. It's your vacation, let the possible bus delays force you to take things easy and go with the flow. The Mediterranean way of life is definitely one that's more easy going, after all.

>TOURIST

13. LEARN ABOUT THE FISHING HISTORY

As a coastal city, Viareggio has a closely linked history with the water. That history and culture didn't always revolve around the beach and relaxing on the sand. The city has a rich fishing culture that is still alive and well. If you walk towards the docks, you'll see plenty of fishing boats coming in and going out to sea with the catch of the day, you can even buy fresh and directly from the fishermen if you're a seafood lover.

If you're curious about this history of Viareggio's fishing culture, head over to Darsena, the old heart of the city. It's just a short walk over a footbridge and you'll be right in the middle of Viareggio's living history. While you're there, you can stop into the Museo della Marineria for some more in depth learning. The small museum costs a few euros to enter, but it's worth it if you like to soak up the local culture while you vacation. Even if you're not a fishing buff, the antique equipment and boat logs will still pique your interest. Trust me.

Be warned, however, while the museum association is making every effort to accommodate visitors of all kinds, most of the information is still only written in Italian. There's still a lot to see and wonder at, but you may need to brush up on your Italian skills to read about it all.

14. BE READY FOR THE HEAT

If you're planning a summer vacation in Viareggio, get ready to deal with heat. Not just any heat, humid heat. Being right on the coast, you'll definitely have moisture in the air all year round, which makes winters cold and humid and summers hot and humid. However, what makes the summer months brutal is the lack of air conditioning in older buildings. Most restaurants and newer hotels and apartments may be equipped with air conditioning units, but older accommodations most likely won't. Get yourself a little fan to take with you and maybe an oscillating floor fan or two if wherever you're staying doesn't have them available. Also, make sure you stay hydrated, when it's that hot and humid, you won't even know how much water you lose and spending your vacation dehydrated is not ideal.

>TOURIST

15. YOU CAN DEFINITELY HOOF IT

Whether you decide you want to rent a car or take public transportation for longer treks is more your speed, Viareggio is definitely a walkable city. All of the sites are within walking distance and the city doesn't spread out so much that would make walking anywhere inaccessible. If you're a fast walker, most of the places you may be looking to get to shouldn't be more than an hour long walk, at most, most things are within 30 minutes distance at a brisk paced walk. It's a great way to see the city and explore so you can make sure you don't miss anything while you're here. If you want to move around a little faster, consider renting a bicycle or a scooter for as long as you need it.

16. DON'T EXPECT MUCH ENGLISH

If you're someone who has traveled around a lot to places that have a different first language than what you're fluent in, you may be used to still being able to use English as your fall-back language to make yourself understood. That's not necessarily the case in Viareggio. Don't get me wrong, it's gotten a lot better. More hotel staff than ever can speak English to at least some degree and a lot of menus and important information usually has an English option, even if the translations aren't always 100% correct.

If you're expecting to be able to verbally speak English, you may want to rethink that. You won't find too many people who can speak it fluently enough to hold a conversation. If you do a little planning, however, you should be fine. Have a translator app or phrase book on hand, learn a few key words before your trip, and exercise a little patience, and you shouldn't have any trouble getting around and getting by.

>TOURIST

17. DRESS UP A LITTLE

Italy is one of the most fashionable countries in the world. It's been the birthplace of countless fashion houses and the Milan Fashion Week is internationally renowned. If you're looking to fit in a little when you visit Viareggio, don't be afraid to dress up a little. While Viareggio is a bit more relaxed compared to some of the bigger cities like Milan, Rome, and even Lucca and Florence, so you don't have to go too far to not stick out. You don't need to wear anything expensive or formal, just some nice jeans, boots, and a shirt (whether a blouse, t-shirt, button-up shirt) and you'll fit right in. Around Viareggio, more important than being fashionable is being presentable. Dress for the season, darker colors in the colder months, brighter colors when it's warmer. The number one rule, though, don't dress too casually, especially for a night, or you'll stick out as a tourist for sure.

18. BUT YOU DON'T HAVE TO EXAGGERATE

Like I said, in Viareggio the general dress code is to look presentable more than needing to worry about looking like you're straight out of a fashion campaign. You don't have to exaggerate. If you love dressing up, go for it, rock your style with confidence. If you're looking to blend in, though, if you dress up too much, you might end up drawing more attention than if you were too dressed down. On Sundays you are more likely to see people walking around in their "Sunday best", that's when you can break out the fancier clothes without too many people batting an eye. The rest of the time? Unless you have dinner plans at a nice restaurant or you're going to an event that would warrant dressing up a little, you might end up risking looking like a different sort of tourist. You might pass as Italian, but from the bigger metropolitan areas more than a complete local.

>TOURIST

19. VISIT THE LAKE

When you visit Viareggio, make sure you head over to Torre del Lago for more than just the Puccini opera history. Torre del Lago literally means tower of the lake, and the lake is beautiful. Massaciuccoli lake is an over four mile wide lake that spans two different municipalities. Some of which is in Viareggio. While much of the wildlife has, sadly, disappeared over the years, you can still find an impressive amount of flora and fauna at any time of the year.

The lake is a great place to spend a relaxing afternoon or morning after the excitement of the rest of your Viareggio trip and can really help you reset and recharge. Puccini found it to be a great place to call home, if one of the masters of the opera world thought it was good enough to call home, that's a great endorsement in my book. Don't expect to go in the water, though, swimming in the lake isn't advised and is even forbidden in most areas.

20. DON'T MISS THE CITTADELLA

Whether you decide to head to Viareggio during Carnevale or not, you should definitely make sure to stop at the Cittadella del Carnevale to learn about its history. The Cittadella is made up of two main parts, the hangars and the museum. During Carnevale, you can sometimes find yourself lucky enough to happen upon the Cittadella when the hangars are open and you can watch the artist teams put their finishing touches on the giant, intricately designed floats.

The museum, on the other hand, is open year round. Tickets are a small fee, just a few euros, that are well worth it if you're interested in the history of Carnevale. You can see small scale models of the winning floats from the Carnevale parades through the years as well as some information into how they're made. It's not an all-day activity, but locals and tourists alike recommend it as a must-visit spot in Viareggio. Museum visiting hours vary between the summer and the winter, however, so make sure to check them before you head over. Also, much like the fishing museum, most of the information is in English at this time, so be prepared to look up some

21. I HOPE YOU LIKE FISH

You can't visit anywhere in Italy without trying local cuisine. I don't mean just pizza and gelato. I mean dishes that are local to where you're visiting, with locally sourced ingredients. In Viareggio, that means fish. It's fishing history and the continued popularity of fishing as both a hobby and a livelihood mean that you'll have plenty of seafood options at basically every restaurant you eat at. Spaghetti allo scoglio, frutti di mare, fritto misto, those are just a few of the seafood options you'll have. Those options and most of the others you'll find are typically shellfish based, so be careful of that and let your servers know if you have an allergy. If you're really opposed to seafood, you'll still have plenty of options, but if you're a fan, or if you're even open to it, you have to have the fish in Viareggio..

22. GO FOR A LONG WALK ON THE BEACH

Picture this, you've had a long, fun day exploring Viareggio, maybe you visited the promenade market, maybe you took in the sites, and before you head to a late dinner, you decide to go for a nice walk. That sounds pretty great, right? You know what would be better? Taking that walk on the beach. The Viareggio sand is soft and easy to walk on, you don't have to worry about sharp rocks or a hilly landscape to make the walk difficult. With its long expanse of beautiful water and sand, you can literally walk for miles and end up in a neighboring town without even realizing it. Taking a long walk on the beach is a great way to relax on vacation, and Viareggio was practically made for doing just that.

>TOURIST

23. CAREFUL OF THE JELLYFISH

If you go to Viareggio during the warmer months, you're going to end up at the beach at least once. It's basically inevitable. However, if you're not used to swimming in the sea or the ocean, you may not be used to having to deal with some of the more treacherous sea creatures. In Viareggio the prime example of that is the jellyfish. Every summer they make themselves known to a few unlucky swimmers. Usually, however, there aren't too many of them and getting stung is rare. You can go an entire summer as a local and never see one once. Other years, however, you'll see dozens over the course of the season. There's really no way to predict what each year will hold as far as the jellyfish population is concerned. Don't be worried. Just keep an eye out and make sure you have a plan in case you or anyone you travel with gets stung.

24. ...AND THE WEEVER FISH

Maybe you're used to jellyfish and how to avoid them, but you want to be aware of another little sea critter that can potentially make your beach day take a turn for the worse. That's the weever fish. Known locally as raganella (don't look that word up, however, you'll be directed to a frog, not a fish), this fish tends to stay tucked under the sand in the shallow parts of the water so they're easily stepped on by unsuspecting swimmers.

Getting stung is rare, but it's definitely something that you should take steps to avoid if you can. How? Shuffle your feet when you walk through the sand to spook any fish that might be lurking around and save yourself the metaphoric and literal pain of dealing with the sting. If you do get stung, don't panic, it hurts, but you'll be fine. Just tell a lifeguard or someone at a beach establishment and they'll get you all set up to take care of it to make the pain pass as quickly as possible. Weever fish have the same sort of toxin as bees, however, so if you're allergic to bees and wasps, be extra careful and make sure to have your medicine with you. Just in case.

>TOURIST
25. GO ON A GELATO CRAWL

You can't go to Italy without expecting to eat your body weight in gelato. That goes for Viareggio as well. The city is full of gelaterie, many of which make their own gelato in house. You know what that means? Set up a little walking gelato tour for yourself. Sample the signature flavor of every location, from the dozens of flavors by Nilo to the award winning rose petal flavor by Galliano. If you visit during the summer, doing a gelato crawl is one sure-fire way to keep you cool, and even in the winter when it's colder, the extra chill is still worth it. You can't get gelato that tastes like it does in Italy anywhere else in the world, and Viareggio's got some famous spots you just have to visit.

26. DON'T EXPECT SNOW

If you've looked at a map during your vacation planning, you may notice that Viareggio is pretty close to the mountains. You'll even notice them in the distance. However, if you visit in the winter, don't expect any snowfall to hit the city, even if the mountains are covered in it. The temperatures near the water are usually too warm for snow. You'll see some frost in the early hours of the morning, and every so often, at most once a year, you'll catch a flurry. Don't look forward to walking down snowy streets or getting into a snowball fight on the beachfront, however. Even if you're lucky enough to visit when snowflakes dust the ground, it usually doesn't last long. The snow melts quickly and doesn't really stick to begin with. Snap a picture and try to enjoy it while it lasts, because it's rare.

>TOURIST

27. GET USED TO THE BUSINESS HOURS

You may have heard something about how Italians like to take things easy and don't like to rush. That carries over to business hours as well. If you're used to 24-hour businesses and being able to get something at all hours of the night because, no matter what, something will be open, you'll have to think again.

There are a few business hour based things you'll want to consider when you visit Viareggio. The first one is based on what time of year you visit. Most restaurants, cafes, and stores will have hours that vary depending on which half of the year it is, often staying open longer from May until the middle or end of September when there are more tourists and more people out and about. It's usually not a drastic difference, but it's still noticeable. Places may stay open an hour or two later in the evening or be closed for less time in the afternoon when it's warmer, or they may change which day during the week they decide to stay closed to take the day off.

You'll also want to be aware of the fact that most businesses will close for a few hours in the afternoon, usually between noon/12:30 and 3 p.m., though specifics do vary depending on location. You also won't find any businesses open later than midnight at the latest, and that's mostly only during the height of the tourist season and only in places that see a lot of foot traffic. All of that is stuff you'll have to consider when you plan out your trip.

28. DON'T SKIP MERENDA

If you want to fit in with the locals, then "merenda" or an afternoon snack, is a must. Italians typically eat dinner later, so it's very common to grab a quick bite in the late afternoon. Often this little snack is sweet in nature. You'll see little groups of co-workers or families stop in at a cafe to get a coffee and a small pastry. Merenda isn't a heavy meal, and it may not be the most encompassing as far as the food groups are concerned, but it's a cozy tradition that the locals love and you will, too.

>TOURIST

29. BE PREPARED TO EAT... A LOT

If you visit Viareggio, don't expect to stick to your diet and don't come with the intention of counting calories if you can help it, because you'll definitely eat a lot while you're here. If you decide to eat your biggest meals at restaurants, you'll likely eat multiple courses, an appetizer, a first course, a main course, and you can't forget dessert. True, portions are smaller here than in some other countries, like the USA, for example, but that's still a lot of food. Not only that, it's good food, so you'll definitely find room for it all. With all the dishes and specialties Viareggio has to offer, and all the different restaurant choices you have at your disposal, you'll be happy to get in all the walking you'll do while you're here because you'll be eating enough for two, or three.

30. BE READY FOR SOME OLD SCHOOL WAYS OF LIFE

Viareggio is an old town, not just in age, but also in its mentality. While it may be more modern and with the times compared to many hamlets in the country, it's still a bit traditional compared to cities like Milan that embrace the modern and being up-to-date. You'll see it a bit in all sorts of aspects of life in Viareggio, and it usually adds a bit of old-school charm to the city, but it can sometimes be an inconvenience. Much of how the city runs is based on older ways of thinking, from operating hours to what language or dietary options are available to people. Viareggio became a hotspot in the mid 1900s, and a lot of that has stuck around. Heck, up until a few years ago, it wasn't surprising to see three star hotels with shared bathrooms for an entire floor of guests. Things are getting modernized, bit by bit, but try to be patient if it's not quite what you're used to.

>TOURIST

31. DON'T RELY ON THE WI-FI

Can you believe there was ever a time before Wi-Fi? It's hard to believe, even if you know you lived without it for years, or decades. Now it's such an integral part of life that when it stops working it feels like you're cut off from the world. It's so commonplace that it's not unheard of to have free access through the city or a business establishment of some sort while you're shopping or eating. While that is still the case in Viareggio, I would recommend not relying on the Wi-Fi and to plan ahead so you don't need it in an emergency. As of right now, the city doesn't have free, wide-spread Wi-Fi and doesn't plan on adding it any time soon. While most hotels will offer at least some access, and many restaurants as well, it's not the sort of connection you can really rely on. With a service that often lags, drops, is insecure, or just won't recognize the supposed correct password, trying to use it to check your email or social media may be more of a headache than it's worth most of the time.

32. TAKE IN A SHOW

While Viareggio may not show up on too many lists as being a top pick for its theater or music scenes, you'll still have plenty of opportunities to take in a show, and, if you have the chance, you definitely should. Between the opera performances during the Puccini celebrations and the local theater troupes will perform shows ranging from The Importance of Being Earnest to The Rocky Horror Picture Show, with spatterings of concerts, ballets, and circus performances in between, there's bound to be something for everyone here. Yes, many of the theater shows will be in Italian, but theater is almost a universal language. If you enjoy the art form, you'll enjoy it in any language! Besides, for being a place where English is less commonly heard compared to other cities, you'll find a surprising amount of shows performed in English as well.

>TOURIST

33. DECIDE YOUR BUDGET BASED ON LOCATION

Like many places, your vacation in Viareggio will be affected in more ways than one by location, location, location. Not only will what area you decide to stay in affect things like parking and how much peace and quiet you'll have, your budget will also likely revolve around where you decide to stay. Viareggio is a safe city, so you don't have to worry much about that when picking your neighborhood, so your lodging's price will be determined mostly based on how far away you'd be from the sites. Namely, the beach, Hotels along the seafront will be notoriously leaps and bounds more expensive than hotels found further inland. The same goes for vacation apartment rentals. These places are completely worth it if being near the action of the seafront and the water are top priorities for you, but if you're ambivalent on the matter or there are other things that are more important to you, then you may want to look elsewhere rather than blow so much of your budget for a location that isn't completely suited for you.

34. HEAD TO CAMAIORE FOR A MOUNTAIN ESCAPE

If you're looking for a quick day-trip you can decide on a last-minute, then head to Camaiore for the day. The city has ancient roman roots compared to Viareggio that was largely wetland during the Roman empire. You can even drive into the mountains for the day if you want to get the best of both worlds while on your vacation. If you're traveling during the Summer, Camaiore will give you a little relief from the heat and the crowds that can gather in Viareggio. Instead, during the winter, you can reach the snow without too much difficulty before heading back to Viareggio to enjoy the rest of your coastal stay. At just a 15 minute drive's distance away, carve out a little time to head to Camaiore, you won't regret it.

>TOURIST
35. SUPPORT A LOCAL ARTIST

Viareggio, and the entire Versilia area, is home to artists of all sorts. Many painters and writers have called this city home over the years, even just temporarily and that tradition has continued to this day. When you visit, you'll likely be on the lookout for some souvenirs to remember your vacation by. Why stick with just a magnet or a t-shirt when you can get something truly special and support an artist in the process? Scattered throughout the city you'll find a few galleries with paintings and sculptures you can admire and purchase, but the markets are also a great place to go to look for local artist pieces to bring home with you. From paintings to jewelry and even the odd locally recorded CD or locally published book, you won't have any trouble finding something that you'll feel like you just have to have that supports a local artist or artisan in the process.

36. PICK YOUR FAVORITE CAFE

No matter how long you stay in Viareggio, you'll want to go to one of Viareggio's many cafes, also known as "bar" in Italian. If you want to have breakfast like a local, you'll stop in for your coffee and a pastry, something light and sweet to get you through the morning. That's not the only time you'll have the opportunity to get yourself a coffee, though. Stop in again mid-morning for a pick-me-up and again for your merenda. Viareggio has hundreds of cafes to choose from, many of which are famous for their home-made pastries, or their coffee, even if you think you found one that's good enough, try a few and pick your favorite. If you're used to paying a pretty penny for a cup at home, the price will also be a nice surprise for your wallet. At less than €2 for a cappuccino, you'll have to force yourself not to drink cup after cup so you don't overdo the caffeine, it's Italian espresso, after all.

>TOURIST

37. HEAD TO THE ARCADE FOR SOME NOSTALGIA

Viareggio is a city that loves its nostalgia. That includes for simpler times when heading to the arcade was all the rage. While in many cities arcades have gone the way of the dinosaur, you'll still find them on the seafront promenade in Viareggio. During the summer you'll see its doors open for people of all ages, whether young or just young at heart, to wander in and kill some time. If you're looking to have an evening of fun that's a little out of the box or you're just looking to tap into the inherent charm and coziness of hanging out at an arcade without a care in the world, then Viareggio has got you covered. The only downside? The arcade is a bit small, if you're used to having tons of options, you may be a bit disappointed. You also might have to do a little translating for games that don't have playing in English as an option, but once you get used to it, you'll just have to worry about letting go and having fun.

38. HAVE AN APERITIVO

If merenda isn't your thing (or even if it is!) you absolutely can't go to Viareggio without having an aperitivo, or a before dinner drink. This tradition is a staple in Italian culture, especially on the weekend, though you'll see people enjoying their aperitivo every day of the week. Since Italians eat dinner so late, and dinner was traditionally a light meal, as you didn't want to eat large amounts of heavy food right before bed, an aperitivo was a perfect little way to hit the spot after work or before your dinner reservations.

Typically consisting of a drink, alcoholic or not, and some snacks, some places in Viareggio really began to outdo themselves. Particularly during the summer months, you'll find bars with large spreads of finger foods and other items you can eat cold that you can nibble on while you enjoy your drink outside. A little inside tip? If you're used to eating dinner early, an aperitivo might be the way to go, often you can eat enough food for an entire meal and you'll be hard pressed to find a restaurant that's open for early diners.

>TOURIST

39. DON'T FORGET THE PIZZA

Any true Viareggino would tell you that you have to go to Rusticanella if you visit. Having been consistently open for decades, it's basically a local institution. While most pizzerias will only allow you to order entire pizzas, Rusticanella lets you buy by the slice. You pay by weight and the slices are large, crunchy, and everything you could ask for from. In fact, if you head over during the typical lunchtime hours, be prepared to wait in line for a while before you can head to the counter. It's a popular spot among students for an after-school bite and older locals alike. If you want a quick, inexpensive, delicious, and local eating experience, then Rusticanella better be on your list.

40. BRING THE WHOLE FAMILY

Viareggio is a vacation destination that is great for the whole family. Unlike some cities, it's not geared towards any singular demographic in particular. Whether you're single, a couple, or a family, of any age, you'll feel at home in Viareggio. There's something for everyone. The city is very family-friendly with a lot of events in particular geared towards younger children, especially during the height of the tourist season and times of the year when school is typically out in many parts of the world. The beaches are fairly shallow for quite a distance so you can let your kiddos play in the water in peace.

Even Carnevale with its crowds is geared towards families. You'll see little kids in costumes dancing around to the music without a care in the world because local parents know that their little ones are safe. Sure, Viareggio isn't Disneyland, but, as far as cities go, it's a safe place with a lot of residential families, so traveling here with kids is a breeze.

>TOURIST
41. WATCH OUT FOR WILD BOAR

While you may not see much in the way of wildlife while in Viareggio, especially on land, you do have to be careful of one particular animal that you might come across if you're in a certain area, namely the park, or near the wooded area of Darsena. Wild boar live in those areas and they don't like being disturbed. While not a problem at most times of day and most times of the year, if you're someone who likes to go for early morning walks or runs, especially during the springtime when the weather is getting warmer, you might run into a wild boar if you're not mindful.

Like most wildlife, the boar don't want to hurt you and typically just want to keep their home and their young safe, so, as a tip, avoid running or in or around wooded areas, especially early in the morning. The beach is so close by, it's the perfect place to get some exercise in. Or opt for a nice meandering walk through the city, instead.

42. GET READY TO TAKE IT EASY

Viareggio is an easy-going city. In a lot of ways. Some of those have been touched on, but it's not all learning to relax and go with the flow. When you're vacationing in Viareggio, it's like everything is designed to force you to slow down and relax. The beach during the summer is there to draw you in so you can relax on the sand. In the winter you'll see a lot of places close early, but that's not a depressing thing, it's a way to push you to take things slow, you don't have to rush, you can spend a cold evening relaxed and cozy where it's warm. The city is perfect for just wandering around because it's almost impossible to get lost. In fact, there's a saying that as long as you know where the beach is, you can find your way to where you need to go. So just dial yourself back a few notches and take your Viareggio days slow and steady.

>TOURIST

43. HAVE SOME SEASONAL TREATS

Not only does Viareggio have delicious staple foods for you to try, but no matter what time of year you visit, you'll have seasonal treats to taste as well. If you come during Carnevale, you'll have cenci (also sometimes called frappe) sweet strips of crispy, fried dough. Around March there are frittelle di riso, which are a sort of donut made with rice that's been cooked in milk that is then worked into a dough, fried, and filled with chocolate or cream. Christmas brings pandoro and panettone, which are sweet bread-type cakes that may not have originated in Viareggio, but are often made in house at the numerous bakeries. In the summer the smoothie shops open offering up a lengthy list of drinks to quench your thirst after a long day at the beach. If you're a foodie, Italy is the place for you, and Viareggio, with its central location, is a great place to try seasonal treats from all over the country.

44. YOU MIGHT FIND CONFETTI EVERYWHERE

You might be tired of hearing about Carnevale by this point, especially when you're itching to go, like I know you are, but when it's such an important part of the culture, it's impossible not to talk about, it leaves its mark everywhere! Sometimes literally. I mean confetti. Part of the Carnevale festivities involves liberal use of throwing confetti. Everywhere. At each other, in the air, at the floats, from balconies. Both at the parade and just throughout the city when the excitement starts to disperse. You'll find confetti in cracks and crannies for months. Don't be surprised if you find some in the crevices of your suitcase when you get back home and hiding in your belongings well after you've unpacked from your trip. It's sort of like sand and glitter, it gets everywhere and it's only mildly easier to clean up.

>TOURIST

45. DON'T EXPECT MANY NON-ITALIAN OPTIONS

Viareggio has tons of restaurants. Whether you want a fancier sit-down sort of restaurant, a quick bite on the go, or anything in between, Viareggio's got you covered. However, if you're coming from a place that has a lot of types of food from all over the world, you might be disappointed by the options. In recent years some more diverse, not strictly Italian food options have started to become available. There are sushi places, and chinese restaurants, there's even bubble tea! However, other types of cuisine are still slow going in their introduction to this particular part of Italy.

You won't be wanting for food, and I'm sure you're fully expecting to eat all Italian food while you're here, but if you're here for a while and you get a craving for something else, you may be out of luck, especially if you can't make it over to a neighboring town where there might be a few more options for you.

46. GET OUT ON THE WATER

If you're not just content with being on the beach, Viareggio has opportunities for you to get out on the water as well! The docks are full of boats available for rent so you can spend a day out on the water. Complete with a captain and any crew you need so all you have to do is sit back and enjoy the ride.

If you decide to rent a beach umbrella for the day or your entire stay, some beach establishments will offer a paddle boat you can use if you're looking for a more low-key way out on the water but aren't keen on swimming being how you get further from the shore. If you're up for adventure, you can even rent a surfboard or sign up for a lesson or two. If you want to get on the water, Viareggio's got options to get you there.

>TOURIST
47. SEE THE LOTUS MARSHES

If you plan to go to Viareggio in late June through mid-July, then have to make the trek over to the nearby town of Massarosa to visit the lotus marshes. While not in Viareggio itself, the marshes are part of the Massaciuccoli lake nature preserve which does bleed into Viareggio, and the two towns melt into each other in ways that you almost can't distinguish, even if you're a local!

While the window of time to visit the lotus flowers is narrow, it's well worth it. A few times every year the nursery that is in charge of growing and maintaining the flowers open up the gate and allow visitors to enter and see the lotus up close, but even during off hours, they're still a sight to be seen! All it takes is a short 20 minute drive and you're there! You'll not only see something truly breathtaking, but you'll also be visiting a hidden gem that not even most locals know about!

48. GO BIRD WATCHING

If you want to spend a day away from the city, the Torre del Lago neighborhood is the way to go. More than that, if bird watching is your idea of a relaxing way to spend a little chunk of time while you unwind, the Massaciuccoli lake is the best option in Versilia. You'll see the regular birds, chickadees and seagulls, but what the lake has that the rest of Viareggio and the entire Versilia area doesn't is the Oasi Lipu, a wildlife reserve that is specifically geared towards birds.

Entry to the reserve is free of charge and can be accessed through Massarosa, a town that shares the Massaciuccoli lake. It's well worth the short drive out. You can walk across the wooden footbridges that allow you access onto the lake so you can enjoy the views and see what special types of bird call the lake home during whatever time of year you're visiting. It's a lesser known attraction that you, usually, really have to be a local to know about. Even if you want to stay in the Viareggio area, you're sure to see some interesting wildlife from the Torre del Lago view of the lake.

>TOURIST

49. BECOME A SOCCER FAN

It's not surprising that soccer is a big deal in Italy. Who your team is is a big deal. However, when you come to Viareggio, you might be even more enticed to get into the sport, depending on when you visit. Every year there is the Viareggio Cup, also known as the "Carnevale Cup" due to its occurrence around the time of Carnevale. Youth soccer teams from all over the country bus into Viareggio to compete in a tournament that lasts two weeks.

During that time you'll see the soccer teams roaming around town between games and you'll see locals cheering on their favorites. It's a wholesome tournament that doesn't get as crazy as the professional league games do, so if the antics that go on with the pros has turned you off to getting into soccer, the Viareggio Cup might be a good way to tip your toe in.

The downside of visiting during the Viareggio Cup? Due to the influx of tourists for Carnevale and the soccer teams, it might be hard to find a place to stay unless you make sure to book well in advance.

50. DON'T BE AFRAID TO CHAT WITH THE LOCALS

At this point, I think Viareggio has sold itself as being a place you should definitely visit, but to round out these tips, here's the most important one. When you're in Viareggio, talk to the locals. They're a social group and love chatting with people who are willing to listen. Sure, they may not know much English, and you may not know much Italian, but, trust me, you'll make due and be able to make yourselves understood. They're a friendly sort, in general, and most will jump at the chance to talk to someone new so they can show off their city.

Ask for tips of where to eat. What to order. What you should visit or see first. You can even ask where you can find souvenirs. This book can help you prepare for your visit and give you some ideas of what to do once you get to Viareggio, but the best way to make sure you get all the inside scoop is to ask! Trust me, the Viareggini love their city and want to help make your visit a special one!

>TOURIST

TOP REASONS TO BOOK THIS TRIP

Cultural Festivities: Viareggio has so many festivities throughout the year, Carnevale being the biggest and most famous of them.

Food: All of Italy is worth visiting for the food, but Viareggio offers northern and southern Italian dishes as well as its own lengthy list of specialties.

Viareggio Homebase: Viareggio has great homey vibes and is perfectly located to be your homebase for day trips to other cities.

OTHER RESOURCES:

Carnevale di Viareggio:
https://viareggio.ilcarnevale.com/

Oasi Lipu Massaciuccoli:
http://www.oasilipumassaciuccoli.org/

Puccini Festival: https://www.puccinifestival.it/

Viareggio Cup: https://www.viareggiocup.com/

Visit Tuscany Viareggio:
https://www.visittuscany.com/en/destinations/viareggio/

Visit Versilia Viareggio:
https://www.visittuscany.com/en/destinations/viareggio/

>TOURIST

PACKING AND PLANNING TIPS

A Week before Leaving

- Arrange for someone to take care of pets and water plants.
- Email and Print important Documents.
- Get Visa and vaccines if needed.
- Check for travel warnings.
- Stop mail and newspaper.
- Notify Credit Card companies where you are going.
- Passports and photo identification is up to date.
- Pay bills.
- Copy important items and download travel Apps.
- Start collecting small bills for tips.
- Have post office hold mail while you are away.
- Check weather for the week.
- Car inspected, oil is changed, and tires have the correct pressure.
- Check airline luggage restrictions.
- Download Apps needed for your trip.

Right Before Leaving

- Contact bank and credit cards to tell them your location.
- Clean out refrigerator.
- Empty garbage cans.
- Lock windows.
- Make sure you have the proper identification with you.
- Bring cash for tips.
- Remember travel documents.
- Lock door behind you.
- Remember wallet.
- Unplug items in house and pack chargers.
- Change your thermostat settings.
- Charge electronics, and prepare camera memory cards.

\>TOURIST

READ OTHER GREATER THAN A TOURIST BOOKS

Greater Than a Tourist- California: 50 Travel Tips from Locals

Greater Than a Tourist- Salem Massachusetts USA 50 Travel Tips from a Local by Danielle Lasher

Greater Than a Tourist United States: 50 Travel Tips from Locals

Greater Than a Tourist- St. Croix US Birgin Islands USA: 50 Travel Tips from a Local by Tracy Birdsall

Greater Than a Tourist- Montana: 50 Travel Tips from a Local by Laurie White

Children's Book: Charlie the Cavalier Travels the World by Lisa Rusczyk Ed. D.

> TOURIST

Follow us on Instagram for beautiful travel images:
http://Instagram.com/GreaterThanATourist

Follow *Greater Than a Tourist* on Amazon.

CZYKPublishing.com

> TOURIST

At *Greater Than a Tourist*, we love to share travel tips with you. How did we do? What guidance do you have for how we can give you better advice for your next trip? Please send your feedback to GreaterThanaTourist@gmail.com as we continue to improve the series. We appreciate your constructive feedback. Thank you.

METRIC CONVERSIONS

TEMPERATURE

110° F — — 40° C
100° F —
90° F — — 30° C
80° F —
70° F — — 20° C
60° F —
50° F — — 10° C
40° F —
32° F — — 0° C
20° F —
10° F — — -10° C
0° F —
-10° F — — -18° C
-20° F — — -30° C

To convert F to C:
Subtract 32, and then multiply by 5/9 or .5555.

To Convert C to F:
Multiply by 1.8 and then add 32.

32F = 0C

LIQUID VOLUME

To Convert:	Multiply by
U.S. Gallons to Liters	3.8
U.S. Liters to Gallons	26
Imperial Gallons to U.S. Gallons	1.2
Imperial Gallons to Liters	4.55
Liters to Imperial Gallons	22

1 Liter = .26 U.S. Gallon
1 U.S. Gallon = 3.8 Liters

DISTANCE

To convert	Multiply by
Inches to Centimeters	2.54
Centimeters to Inches	39
Feet to Meters	.3
Meters to Feet	3.28
Yards to Meters	91
Meters to Yards	1.09
Miles to Kilometers	1.61
Kilometers to Miles	.62

1 Mile = 1.6 km
1 km = .62 Miles

WEIGHT

1 Ounce = .28 Grams
1 Pound = .4555 Kilograms
1 Gram = .04 Ounce
1 Kilogram = 2.2 Pounds

\>TOURIST

TRAVEL QUESTIONS

- Do you bring presents home to family or friends after a vacation?
- Do you get motion sick?
- Do you have a favorite billboard?
- Do you know what to do if there is a flat tire?
- Do you like a sun roof open?
- Do you like to eat in the car?
- Do you like to wear sun glasses in the car?
- Do you like toppings on your ice cream?
- Do you use public bathrooms?
- Did you bring a cell phone and does it have power?
- Do you have a form of identification with you?
- Have you ever been pulled over by a cop?
- Have you ever given money to a stranger on a road trip?
- Have you ever taken a road trip with animals?
- Have you ever gone on a vacation alone?
- Have you ever run out of gas?

- If you could move to any place in the world, where would it be?
- If you could travel anywhere in the world, where would you travel?
- If you could travel in any vehicle, which one would it be?
- If you had three things to wish for from a magic genie, what would they be?
- If you have a driver's license, how many times did it take you to pass the test?
- What are you the most afraid of on vacation?
- What do you want to get away from the most when you are on vacation?
- What foods smell bad to you?
- What item do you bring on ever trip with you away from home?
- What makes you sleepy?
- What song would you love to hear on the radio when you're cruising on the highway?
- What travel job would you want the least?
- What will you miss most while you are away from home?
- What is something you always wanted to try?

>TOURIST

- What is the best road side attraction that you ever saw?
- What is the farthest distance you ever biked?
- What is the farthest distance you ever walked?
- What is the weirdest thing you needed to buy while on vacation?
- What is your favorite candy?
- What is your favorite color car?
- What is your favorite family vacation?
- What is your favorite food?
- What is your favorite gas station drink or food?
- What is your favorite license plate design?
- What is your favorite restaurant?
- What is your favorite smell?
- What is your favorite song?
- What is your favorite sound that nature makes?
- What is your favorite thing to bring home from a vacation?
- What is your favorite vacation with friends?
- What is your favorite way to relax?
- Where is the farthest place you ever traveled in a car?

- Where is the farthest place you ever went North, South, East and West?
- Where is your favorite place in the world?
- Who is your favorite singer?
- Who taught you how to drive?
- Who will you miss the most while you are away?
- Who if the first person you will contact when you get to your destination?
- Who brought you on your first vacation?
- Who likes to travel the most in your life?
- Would you rather be hot or cold?
- Would you rather drive above, below, or at the speed limited?
- Would you rather drive on a highway or a back road?
- Would you rather go on a train or a boat?
- Would you rather go to the beach or the woods?

>TOURIST

TRAVEL BUCKET LIST

1.

2.

3.

4.

5.

6.

7.

8.

9.

10.

>TOURIST

NOTES

Printed in Great Britain
by Amazon